W9-AZP-229

# BATS

# BATS

by Sylvia A. Johnson

Photographs by Modoki Masuda

## A Lerner Natural Science Book

Lerner Publications Company ▪ Minneapolis

Sylvia A. Johnson, Series Editor

*Translation of original text by Wesley M. Jacobsen*

*The publisher wishes to thank Merlin Tuttle, Curator of Mammals, Milwaukee Public Museum, and President of Bat Conservation International, for his assistance in the preparation of this book.*

*Photographs on pp. 7 (upper and lower left), 14, 15, 38, 40, and 44 by Merlin D. Tuttle, Bat Conservation International, Milwaukee Public Museum. Drawings by Masayuki Yabuuchi.*

The scientific and common names of bats are explained on page 46. On the following page is a glossary giving definitions and pronunciations of words shown in **bold type** in the text.

LIBRARY OF CONGRESS CATALOGING IN PUBLICATION DATA

**Johnson, Sylvia A.**
   Bats.

   (A Lerner natural science book)
   Adaptation of Kōmori/by Modoki Masuda.
   Includes index.
   Summary: Describes the varied characteristics and habits of bats and the importance of their roles as pollinators and seed dispersers.
   1. Bats—Juveniie literature. [1. Bats] I. Masuda, Modoki, ill. II. Masuda, Modoki. Kōmori. III. Title. IV. Series.
QL737.C5J55  1985        599.4        85-15999
ISBN 0-8225-1461-3 (lib. bdg.)

This edition first published 1985 by Lerner Publications Company.
Text copyright © 1985 by Lerner Publications Company.
Photographs copyright © 1984 by Modoki Masuda.
Text adapted from BATS copyright © 1984 by Modoki Masuda.
English language rights arranged by Japan Foreign-Rights Centre for Akane Shobo Publishers, Tokyo, Japan.

International Standard Book Number: 0-8225-1461-3
Library of Congress Catalog Number: 85-15999

  2  3  4  5  6  7  8  9  10  91  90  89  88  87  86

Dark shapes glide through the night sky on silent wings, their sinister shadows outlined against the light of a full moon. Swooping down to the earth, they hover near houses and deserted buildings, breaking the peace of the night with their disturbing presence. Carriers of disease, drinkers of blood, companions of witches and demons, bats—the very word brings a shiver of fear to most people.

## MAMMALS THAT FLY

This popular image of bats is based on beliefs that are confused, contradictory, and almost all false. As we shall see, very few bats carry disease or feed on blood. The truth about bats, however, also tends to be confusing and full of contradictions.

Many bats are tiny animals no bigger than a hummingbird, but some bats have wing spans as wide as six feet (4 meters). Large numbers of bats eat insects, while others thrive on a diet of fruit, nectar, and even fish. Many bats make their homes in caves, attics, and other dark and hidden places, but some roost right out in the open, in the branches of trees.

Bats make up a varied group of animals, but all bats have some basic things in common. The two most important facts about bats and the two characteristics that make them unique are that they are mammals and that they can fly. Like dogs, horses, gorillas, and humans, bats have hairy bodies, bear live young, and feed their young on milk produced by **mammary glands.** Unlike other mammals, however, they can escape the gravity of the earth and soar on widespread wings, like insects and birds.

Shown here are four of the nearly 1,000 species of bats. Upper left: The head of a leaf-nosed bat *(Hipposideros commersoni)*. Upper right: A hibernating horseshoe bat *(Rhinolophus cornutus)*. Left: A silver-haired bat *(Lasionycteris noctivagans)*. Below: A bent-winged bat *(Miniosterus schreibersii)*.

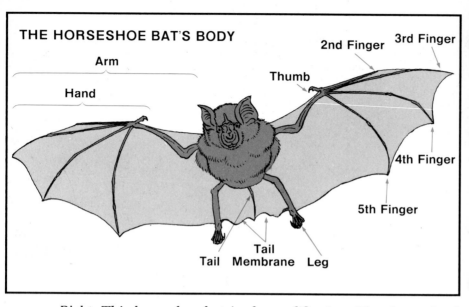

**THE HORSESHOE BAT'S BODY**

Arm

Hand

Thumb

2nd Finger

3rd Finger

4th Finger

5th Finger

Tail

Tail Membrane

Leg

Right: This horseshoe bat is shown life size. The tiny animal weighs only about 1/4 ounce (6 grams).

Let's take a close look at the marvelous wings that enable a bat to take to the sky. The bat shown here is a horseshoe bat from Asia, but it has the same basic wing structure as bats that live in North America and all other parts of the world.

The photograph reveals one important thing about a bat's wings, and that is that they are not made of feathers. Unlike birds, bats fly on wings made of a membrane consisting of two thin layers of skin. This membrane extends out from the sides of a bat's furry body and is supported by the bones of the animal's hands and arms.

It may surprise you to hear that bats have hands, but they

definitely do. In fact, the scientific order that bats belong to is called **Chiroptera,** which means "hand-wing." A bat's hand is much like a human hand, made up of four long fingers and one short thumb that can be easily moved. Compared to a human hand, however, a bat's hand is very large in proportion to the animal's small body.

The long bones of a bat's hand are like the spokes of an umbrella over which is stretched the thin membrane of the wings. The membrane is also attached to the bat's legs and, in the horseshoe bat, to the small tail. (The tails of some other bats are not connected to the wing membrane.)

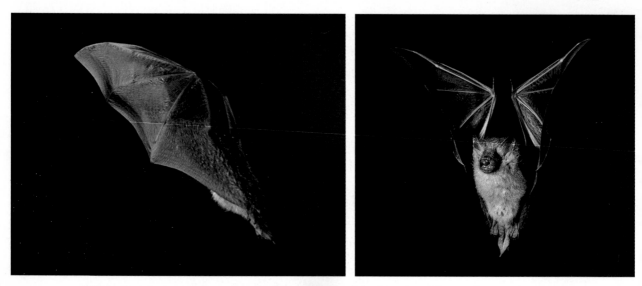

With the help of its remarkable wings, this bat is able to hover in midair. The sideview (left) shows how the shape of the wing membrane is controlled by the bat's fingers.

When a bat is in flight, the thin wing membrane is pulled tight by the bones of its hands. By moving the bones individually, even the small bones that make up the fingers, a bat can quickly change the shape of its wings and the tension of the membrane. This ability gives the flying mammals great maneuverability, enabling them to hover, dive, and turn more easily than most birds.

When a bat folds its wings, the membrane does not become loose and baggy, as does the covering of a folded umbrella. Instead, it forms thousands of little wrinkles or puckers that in effect shrink the area of the wings. These puckers are created by the pulling action of tiny muscles located between the two layers of the wing membrane. Also located in this area are the blood vessels and nerves that nourish the wings and make possible their amazing maneuvers.

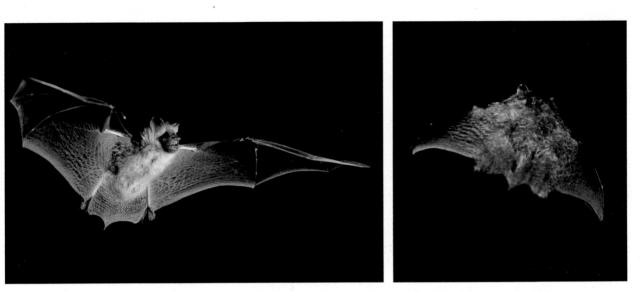

Above left: A bat with its wings and tail membrane fully extended.
Above right: In this view from the back, you can see how the wing membrane is joined to the bat's furry body.

Left: The tiny wrinkles that "shrink" a bat's wings. Below: The network of blood vessels within the wing membrane.

Left: A bat uses the powerful claws on its feet to cling to a tree branch. Right: This bat is hanging by one foot and grooming itself with the other.

Bats are remarkable fliers, but they can also do some pretty amazing things when not in the air. They can crawl on all fours, sleep upside down for hours at a time, and even give themselves a good cleaning while dangling by one foot.

When it is not in flight, a bat's normal position is head down. Almost all other activities of the animal's life are performed while it hangs by its toes from a ledge of rock or a tree branch. A bat's toes are long and strong and equipped with sharp, curved claws. They can get a tight grip in the smallest crack or crevice in a rock wall. A bat's hold on its roost is so powerful that it may not be broken even when the animal dies.

Above: Like this long-eared bat *(Plecotus auritus)*, many bats can crawl along cave walls or ceilings using their thumbs and feet. Right: A long-eared bat grooms its wings with its mouth. Bats are very clean animals and spend a lot of time grooming their fur and their delicate wing membrane.

A frog-eating bat *(Trachops cirrhosus)* swoops down on a frog near a pond in Panama.

This hammer-headed fruit bat *(Hypsignathus monstrosus)* is ready to dine on a ripe tropical fruit.

## THE NIGHT IS FOR EATING

Flying with hand-wings, hanging by their toes: almost all bats have these habits in common. One other characteristic is shared by bats all over the world, and that is being active primarily at night. Bats are **nocturnal** creatures. They spend the day grooming, resting, and sleeping and the nighttime hours searching for food.

What kind of food a bat searches for at night depends on the bat. Bats have quite a variety of eating habits. One group of bats that live in tropical areas of Africa and Asia feeds only on fruits and flower nectar. These large bats, commonly called fruit bats, make up the suborder **Megachiroptera**—the "big hand-wings." Some fruit bats are also called flying foxes because of the foxlike look of their faces.

The fruit-eating bats make up only a small part of the family of bats. Most of the nearly 1,000 species of bats dine on different kind of fare. Some are carnivorous, eating frogs, lizards, birds, and fish. One very small group (about one-third of one percent of all bats) lives on the blood of animals. Many feed on night-flying insects. Because the insect-eating bats and their relatives are generally smaller than the fruit bats, scientists have placed them in the second suborder of bats, **Microchiroptera**—the "little hand-wings."

Around 70 percent of all bats are insect-eaters. If you live in the United States or in any part of the world with a temperate climate, these are the kinds of bats you will probably see around your house and yard.

Moths, beetles, flies, mosquitoes, and many other night-flying insects become meals for hungry bats. The flying mammals usually catch their prey in the air. Sometimes they seize the insects in their mouths. At other times, bats use their wings or the membrane around their tails as a kind of net to scoop the insects up. Small insects are eaten in flight; larger ones may be taken to a roost and consumed while the bat hangs by one foot and uses the other to hold its meal up to its mouth.

A tube-nosed bat *(Murina leucogaster)* munches on an insect while hanging by its thumbs. The bat is using its tail membrane as a kind of napkin to keep its meal from falling to the ground.

## NAVIGATING BY SOUND

Since insect-eating bats seek their prey at night, you might assume that they are keen-eyed hunters like owls and other night-time predators. Many bats actually do have good vision (contrary to legend, there are no blind bats), but most do not depend on their eyesight to guide them in the dark hours of the night.

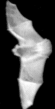

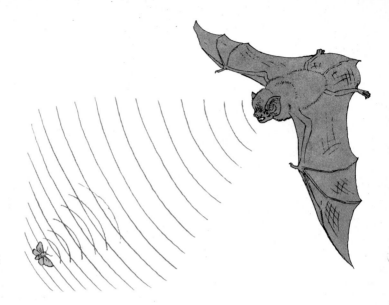

By means of echoloca-
tion, bats can find their
prey on the darkest night.

How then do night-hunting bats find their way around and locate their prey? They use a remarkable system called **echolocation** that is based not on sight but on sound. Bats emit sounds that strike objects and come back as echoes. By interpreting these echoes, the animals can apparently tell what the object is, where it is located, how fast it is moving, and many other facts.

As a hunting bat cruises through the night sky, it sends out pulses of sound at regular intervals. The sounds are high in frequency and usually beyond the range of human hearing. When the sound pulses bounce back from an object that is the appropriate size and shape for a meal, the bat heads in the direction from which the echoes came. At the same time, it begins to send out short sound pulses rapidly, as often as 170 pulses per second. The returning echoes usually enable the bat to home in on the object of its pursuit, even if it is as tiny as a single mosquito or gnat.

The bent-wing bat emits its echolocating sounds through its mouth.

The sounds that a bat makes are produced by its larynx, the same organ that produces sound in humans and other mammals. Some bats emit sounds through their mouths, just as humans do. Others send out sound pulses through their noses. This fact helps to explain the very unusual noses possessed by some species of bats.

The horseshoe bat and many other kinds of bats have what scientists call **nose leaves**, flaps and folds of skin around their nostrils. These strange-looking structures seem to direct and focus the sound pulses sent through the bat's nose. They may also help to keep the sound away from the animal's ears.

Whether they emit sound through their noses or mouths, bats that use echolocation often have large, mobile ears to pick up the returning echoes. Most fruit bats do not use this system of navigation, and they tend to have small ears. These bats usually find their way and their food by sight, and their large, bulging eyes are signs of their excellent vision. Fruit bats also seem to use smell to locate ripe fruit. They have large, long noses but without the exotic decorations of some of their echolocating relatives.

Right and above: The head of a horse-shoe bat. Like many bats that send out sound pulses through their noses, the horseshoe bat has an elaborate nose leaf. It also has the large ears common to bats that use echolocation.

1. Ear; 2-4. Lobes of nose leaf; 5. Mouth; 6. Nostril; 7. Eye

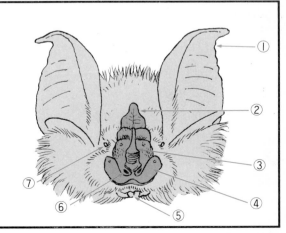

A horseshoe bat awakens from its winter rest and gets ready to resume its active life.

## THE CYCLE OF THE SEASONS

The lives of all bats are influenced by the environments in which they live, but bats in the temperate parts of the world are particularly affected by their surroundings. These bats go through a yearly cycle that is controlled by the changing of the seasons. Let's follow some bats through that cycle to learn about the pattern of their lives.

For bats as for all creatures in temperate climates, spring is a time of reawakened life. In spring, bats emerge from the caves and other protected places where they have spent the winter. After long months of fasting, they are in need of a good meal of insects.

Female bats emerging in spring have a particularly important task ahead of them. In addition to strengthening themselves with food, they must get ready to give birth to the young bats developing inside their bodies.

22

Two horseshoe bats emerge from the cave where they have spent the winter.

In late spring and early summer, pregnant female bats (opposite) find shelter in special nursery caves (left). Here they will bear and rear their young.

The females mated with male bats more than six months ago, before they began their winter's rest. The males' sperm remained stored inside the females' bodies until spring, when fertilization took place and the baby bats began to develop. Now the young bats will be born at a time of year when there is plenty of food for their mothers and for themselves.

The pregnant females of many kinds of bats go to special **nursery caves** to give birth to their young. Thousands or even millions of bats will gather in these sheltered places, which are used by the same species year after year. In most species, male bats do not roost in the nursery caves or help the females in the job of rearing their families.

Young bats in temperate climates are usually born in June or July after developing in their mothers' bodies for about 16 weeks. In most species, each female gives birth to one baby, although in some North American species such as the big brown bat *(Eptesicus fuscus)*, twins, triplets, and even quadruplets may be produced.

Right: This hairless baby bat has just been born. Hanging by her feet, the mother supports the little bat with her wings and tail membrane until it is able to get a grip on her body. Below: This bat is only a few days old, but it is able to cling to the rock with its tiny, curved claws.

Left: A young horseshoe bat nursing. A female bat's two nipples are located on the sides of her body, one under each wing. Right: Female horseshoe bats also have two false nipples, which provide additional anchoring points for clinging young bats.

The first thing that a baby bat does after birth is to find one of its mother's nipples and begin sucking. It needs the nourishment provided by the rich milk, but it also needs something to hang onto so that it does not lose its grip on its mother's body and fall to the cave floor. In some species of bats like the horseshoe bat, the females have two false "nipples" in addition to the ones that produce milk. These nipples, located on the lower part of the female's body, give the baby bat another place to anchor it-self when it is not nursing.

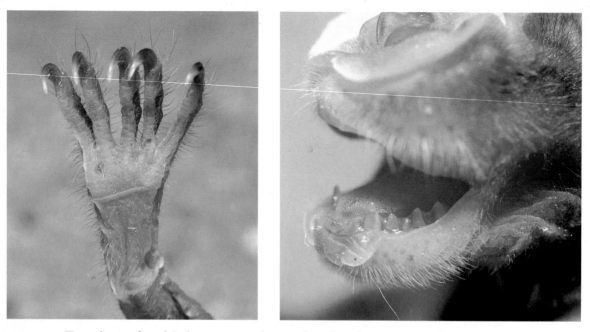

Ten days after birth, a young horseshoe bat has strong claws on its feet (left) and sharp little teeth in its mouth (right).

Because hanging on is so important to a young bat's life, the little animal is born with features that enable it to get a good grip on things. Its feet and legs are large and strong, and the claws are well developed. A young bat's teeth also develop quickly, allowing it to cling tightly to its mother's nipples. Its wings, on the other hand, are weak and will not be capable of flight for more than a month.

If a baby bat does lose hold of its mother's body and fall to the cave floor, it will probably not survive. Even if the fall does not kill it, the mother bat is often not able to pick her large baby up and carry it back to her roost.

Above: Baby horseshoe bats clinging to their mothers as they hang from a cave roof. Right: This young bat has died after losing its grip and falling to the cave floor.

A cluster of hairless young bent-wing bats hanging from a cave roof

Of course, baby bats cannot spend all their lives clinging to their mothers' bodies. The females must leave their young from time to time in order to get the food they need for themselves.

When a mother bat goes out to hunt, she leaves her baby hanging from the cave wall or roof. The female comes back for short periods during the night to nurse the baby and then goes out again to find another nourishing meal of insects. While its mother is gone, the young bat hangs in a tightly packed cluster with other youngsters, all crowded together to keep warm.

If it is necessary to move a young bat to another roost or to a place of safety, the mother flies with the baby clinging to the front of her body. Female bats have been seen carrying youngsters that are almost as big as they are themselves.

A group of young horseshoe bats "calling" their mothers by emitting high-frequency sounds

In many nursery caves, there may be thousands of young bats hanging on the walls, waiting for the return of their hunting mothers. How does a female bat recognize her own offspring in the midst of so many?

Apparently, many mother bats recognize their young by sound. When females return to the nursery cave, the young bats emit high-frequency sounds, just as hunting bats do. A mother bat seems to know the sound of her own baby's "voice" and flies toward it. To make sure that she has found the right youngster, the mother also smells and licks the baby. Only then does she allow the hungry little bat to begin nursing.

This series of photographs shows a female horseshoe bat picking out her own baby among the thousands in a nursery cave. Attracted by her youngster's voice, the mother approaches a group of babies (left). She licks a young bat to make sure that it is hers (center) and then allows the baby to nurse (right).

Nourished by their mothers' milk, young bats grow rapidly, becoming larger and stronger every day. Their naked skin is soon covered with a coat of fine, light-colored fur that gradually changes to the color of the adults of their species. Their wings expand, and the youngsters often exercise them by flapping while hanging from their roosts. In this way, they practice for the flights they will soon be making.

As the young bats get bigger, their mothers leave them alone for longer periods of time, returning occasionally to nurse their offspring. It will not be long before they will stop feeding milk to their big babies, and the youngsters will have to find their own food on the wing.

These horseshoe bats have been weaned from their mothers' milk and are ready to try hunting on their own.

Left: **This group of horseshoe bats includes brown adult females and their young. One month old, the youngsters are still wearing their greyish baby fur.** Right: **A young horseshoe bat practices flying inside the nursery cave.**

About three to five weeks after they are born, most young bats are ready for a little independence. They start making practice flights around the nursery cave and eventually venture out into the dark night along with their mothers. The young bats begin to hunt, probably with some help and guidance from the older generation. Soon they are feeding themselves on the diet appropriate to their particular species.

During the rest of the summer, the young bats and their mothers spend their days resting in the nursery cave and their nights hunting for food. They eat as much as they can during this period because they will need all the energy they can get in the coming weeks. Both the adult females and their young offspring are about to enter into a new phase of their lives.

In the autumn, the young bats and their mothers leave the nursery caves for the last time. They must find suitable places in which to spend the cold months of winter.

Some species of bats migrate, like birds, to areas where the climate is warmer. For example, Mexican free-tailed bats *(Tadarida brasiliensis mexicana)* use nursery caves in the southwestern United States and spend the winter in central Mexico, where they can continue feeding on insects. These bats migrate as much as 1,500 miles (2,500 kilometers) to reach their warm winter homes. Other bats make equally long journeys, perhaps guided by inherited instincts or by older bats that have made the trips in previous years.

Many bats in temperate areas do not escape to warmer climates but spend the winter in their home territories. These bats survive the cold by **hibernation.**

Most bats do not hibernate in the same caves where they raise their young. Instead they seek out different shelters that have conditions just right for hibernation—calm air, high humidity, and steady temperatures that stay a little above freezing. In these caves, or **hibernacula,** bats of all ages, both sexes, and several species gather together. With their wings folded, they hang alone or in clusters on the walls and roofs.

As the winter weather becomes colder, the bats' body temperature falls until it is close to the freezing mark. Their heart rates slow down from 400 beats a minute to below 25 beats per minute. All the rest of their bodily functions slow down as well,

With their wings wrapped snugly around them, two horseshoe bats begin their winter's hibernation.

and the animals become completely inactive. They will live through the winter on the food energy stored during the summer months of busy eating. When spring comes, they will be ready to take up the active cycle of their lives once again.

The dwarf epauletted bat *(Micropteropus pusillus)* lives in Africa, where it feeds on wild figs and other fruits.


BATS IN TROPICAL REGIONS

Hundreds of kinds of bats inhabit the tropical regions of the world, where there is no cold winter and no need to hibernate. The lives of these bats have the same basic pattern all year round. Days are spent roosting in trees, caves, or other sheltered places and the nights feeding on fruits or flowers.

Since the tropical year is like one long summer in temperate climates, there are plants blooming and bearing fruit at all times. Bats in the tropics are not usually faced with a severe shortage of food, although they may have to move to a different area to find a food supply. Thus they have the energy to remain active throughout the year, sometimes even producing young twice in a single year.

In their search for food, tropical bats that eat nectar and fruit perform a great service for the human race. Nectar-feeding bats carry pollen from flower to flower, just as bees and butterflies do. In many areas of the tropics, bats are important pollinators of forest trees and plants. Bats that eat fruit often swallow the seeds and then eliminate them while in flight. In this way, they distribute the seeds over large areas, making possible the development of new plants.

In their roles as pollinators and seed dispersers, bats have contributed to the growth of many valuable tropical plants, including bananas, dates, figs, avocados, cashews, and cloves. Today, many of the cultivated forms of these plants are raised on plantations where human efforts have replaced the work of bats. The wild plants, however, are still vital because they are often used to breed new varieties of cultivated forms that are healthier or more productive. These and hundreds of other wild tropical plants depend on hungry bats for their growth and pollination.

In taking nectar from a banana flower, this short-nosed bat *(Cynopterus sphinx)* picks up pollen that it carries to the flowers of other wild banana plants.

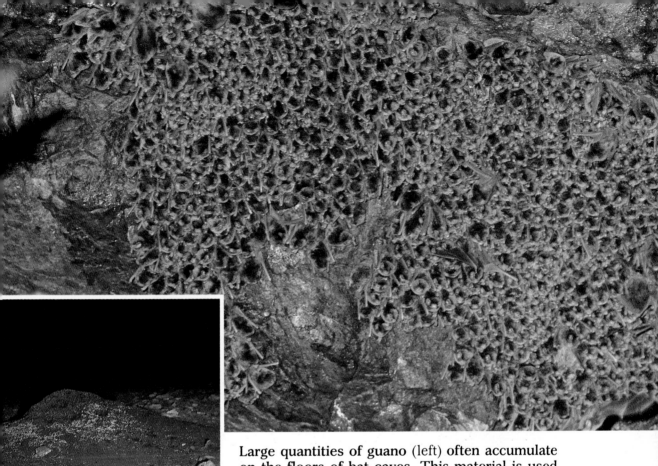

Large quantities of guano (left) often accumulate on the floors of bat caves. This material is used as a fertilizer in many parts of the world.

## BATS AND PEOPLE

Distributing pollen and seeds is only one of the ways that bats benefit people. Insect-eating bats devour millions of insects, including such harmful or pesky kinds as mosquitoes. Bat droppings, called **guano,** are often used as fertilizer, and bat caves in many parts of the world, including the southwestern United States, have been mined for this valuable material.

41

Bats have also proved to be very useful subjects for scientific research. As mammals, they have much in common with human beings, and their long life spans—30 years or more in some species—make it possible to use them in long-range research programs.

Scientific studies of some of the bat's own special features have already led to important medical breakthroughs. For example, research on the animals' echolocation system has made it possible to develop navigational aids for blind people that make use of echoes from sound pulses. The female bat's unique ability to store sperm in her body has been the source of new information in the study of human fertility.

Bats do a great deal of good for people, but many people do not return the favor to their fellow mammals. In some parts of the world, bats are hated and persecuted because of false beliefs about their habits.

The most damaging of the false ideas about bats is that they are dirty animals that transmit diseases to humans. In fact, bats are very clean in their habits, and there is no evidence at all that they are a major source of human disease.

Bats do get rabies, as do most mammals, but they very seldom give the disease to people. Statistics show that in the last 30 years, only 10 people in the United States have died of rabies from bats. Unlike some animals, rabid bats are not aggressive. A bat sick with rabies will bite, however, if it is disturbed or handled. Therefore it is not a good idea to pick up a bat that you see lying on the ground or in some other open place. Such a bat is most likely sick and should be left alone.

A bat demonstrates its amazing echolocation system by flying through a complex pattern of thin wire. Studies of echolocation have enabled scientists to develop devices to aid blind people.

Wrinkled-lipped bats *(Tadarida plicata)* leaving a cave in Thailand. When their caves are destroyed or invaded by humans, bats are deprived of the shelter that is essential to their lives.

Because so many people dislike and fear bats, the animals are often the targets of human efforts to destroy them or the places where they live. In some parts of the United States, the entrances to bat caves have been dynamited to prevent their inhabitants from entering or leaving. The destruction of just one cave can deprive millions of bats of essential shelter. Some species of bats are even now on the brink of extinction because their living places have been destroyed by unthinking people.

Even when people enter hibernating or nursery caves, they can unintentionally cause serious damage. Bats aroused from hibernation use up much valuable food energy and may not have enough left to survive the winter. When females with young are disturbed, they may be forced to flee and leave their helpless babies behind. Exploring bat caves may seem to be a harmless pasttime, but it can have disastrous results for the bats.

A more direct attack on bats is made by some farmers in tropical countries who kill the animals because they feed on fruits in their orchards. They do not realize that the good bats do in pollinating and dispersing seeds far outweighs any damage they may cause to crops.

There *are* places where bats are not persecuted by humans. In England and in many European countries, the animals are widely recognized as beneficial, and people build bat "houses" in yards and parks to attract the flying mammals. Only when human beings all over the world understand how much good bats do and how little harm will these gentle and fascinating animals be free to live their quiet lives in peace and safety.

# THE NAMES OF BATS

Wrinkled-lipped bat, tube-nosed bat, hammer-headed fruit bat, greater mustache bat—these are just a few of the strange-sounding English names given to different kinds of bats. In other languages, bats have names that are equally exotic and probably just as hard to remember.

Such names are known as common names because they are the names often used by non-scientists to refer to bats. Common names are usually based on some conspicuous physical feature or habit of an animal. They are not a very reliable means of identification, however, because there may be several animals with similar characteristics and they may all end up with the same common name. For example, there are many bats throughout the world commonly known as leaf-nosed bats because, as we have seen, a nose leaf is a very common bat feature.

If you want to find out about a particular leaf-nosed bat, the only sure way to identify it is by its scientific name. This two-part name in Latin or Greek is the one recognized and used by scientists everywhere. It refers to the bat's species, its group within the system of scientific classification, and is given on the basis of similarities in structures and features shared by all members of the group. If you can call a leaf-nosed bat by its species name—*Asellia tridens*, for example—then you will have no trouble identifying it among the hundreds of other leaf-nosed bats in the world.

In this book, the scientific name of each kind of bat is given when the species is first mentioned in caption or text.

46

# GLOSSARY

**Chiroptera (ki-RAHP-ter-uh)**—the scientific order to which bats belong

**echolocation**—a system of navigation in which sounds sent out by bats come back as echoes that are interpreted to supply information about the location, distance, and size of objects in the animals' environment

**guano (GWAHN-oh)**—the droppings of bats, used as fertilizer. The word can also refer to the droppings of sea birds, which are used for a similar purpose

**hibernacula (hi-buhr-NAK-yu-luh)**—caves and other sheltered places where hibernating animals spend the winter

**hibernation**—a state of inactivity during which heart beat, respiration, and other bodily functions slow down

**mammary (MAM-uh-ree) glands**—glands that produce milk in mammals

**Megachiroptera (meg-uh-ki-RAHP-ter-uh)**—one of the two suborders of bats, made up of large bats that eat fruit and flower nectar

**Microchiroptera (my-kro-ki-RAHP-ter-uh)**—one of the two suborders of bats, made up of small bats most of which eat insects

**nocturnal**—active primarily at night

**nose leaves**—the flaps and folds of skin and tissue around the noses of bats that navigate by echolocation

**nursery caves**—caves where female bats go to bear and raise their young

# INDEX

89-12

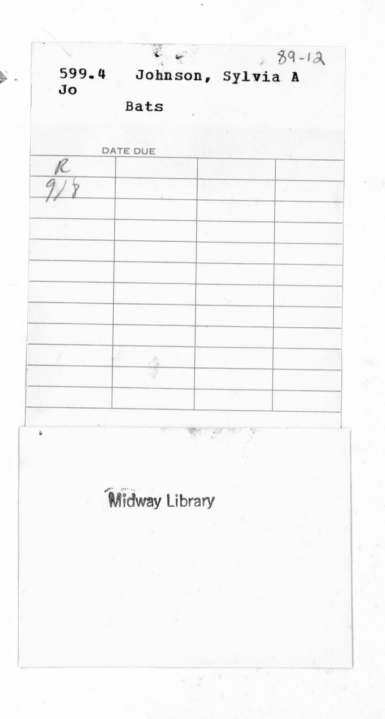

89-12

599.4     Johnson, Sylvia A
Jo
        Bats

| DATE DUE | | | |
|---|---|---|---|
| R 9/8 | | | |
| | | | |
| | | | |
| | | | |
| | | | |
| | | | |
| | | | |
| | | | |
| | | | |
| | | | |
| | | | |
| | | | |